Discover India
City by City

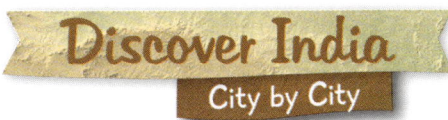

MUMBAI
Here we come

SONIA MEHTA

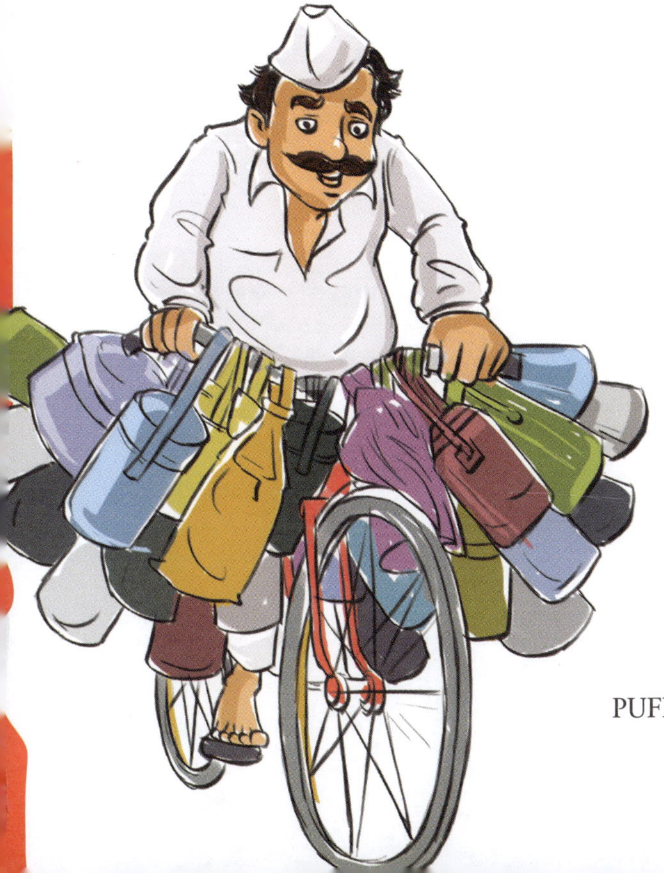

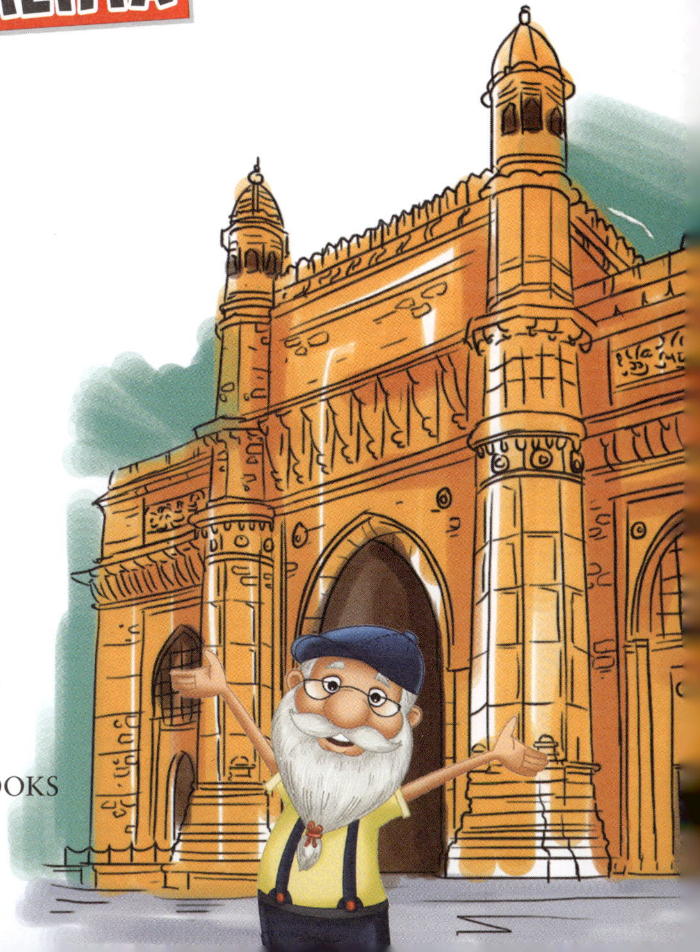

PUFFIN BOOKS

PUFFIN BOOKS

USA | Canada | UK | Ireland | Australia | New Zealand | India | South Africa | China | Singapore

Puffin Books is part of the Penguin Random House group of companies whose addresses can be found at global.penguinrandomhouse.com

Published by Penguin Random House India Pvt. Ltd
4th Floor, Capital Tower 1, MG Road,
Gurugram 122 002, Haryana, India

First published in Puffin Books by Penguin Random House India 2018

Picture Credits

P 8: Old map of the seven islands of Mumbai (© TIFR, Nichalp [GFDL (http://www.gnu.org/copyleft/fdl.html) or CC-BY-SA-3.0 (http://creativecommons.org/licenses/by-sa/3.0/)], via Wikimedia Commons); P 10: Powai Lake (© Udaykumar PR [CC BY 3.0 (https://creativecommons.org/licenses/by/3.0)], via Wikimedia Commons), A flooded street in Mumbai (arun sambhu mishra/Shutterstock.com); P 12: Chowpatty (TK Kurikawa/Shutterstock.com); P 17: Bombay Harbour (© G41rn8 [CC BY-SA 4.0 (https://creativecommons.org/licenses/by-sa/4.0)], from Wikimedia Commons) P 19: Dhobi Ghat (wantanddo/Shutterstock.com); P 20: Mount Mary Church (EQRoy/Shutterstock.com); P 22: Kanehri Caves (arun sambhu mishra/Shutterstock.com); P 23: Crawford Market (bodom/Shutterstock.com); P 25: Sassoon Dock AnilD/Shutterstock.com; P 29: Ballard Estate (Snehal Jeevan Pailkar/Shutterstock.com); P 30: Mahim Fort (© Nicholas (Nichalp) [CC BY-SA 3.0 (https://creativecommons.org/licenses/by-sa/3.0)], from Wikimedia Commons); P 31: Chor Bazaar (Pete Burana/Shutterstock.com), Antique shop, Chor Bazaar (Kalcutta/Shutterstock.com); P 33: A beach in Mumbai (Pete Burana/Shutterstock.com); P 36: Crawford Market (Snehal Jeevan Pailkar/Shutterstock.com); P 37: A miniature double decker bus, BEST Mueseum (© Bishnupriya Sen); P 38: Auto rickshaw driver (Marben/Shutterstock.com); P 39: Chhatrapati Shivaji Maharaj Airport (Tukaram.Karve/Shutterstock.com); P 40: Khotachiwadi Backstreets and chawls (© urbzoo [CC BY 2.0 (https://creativecommons.org/licenses/by/2.0)], via Wikimedia Commons); P 42: Brabourne Stadium (FiledIMAGE/Shutterstock.com); P 44: RK Studio (© Anto Libin [CC BY-SA 3.0 (https://creativecommons.org/licenses/by-sa/3.0)], from Wikimedia Commons); P 51: Bademiya (© Benjamin Vander Steen from Victoria, Canada [CC BY 2.0 (https://creativecommons.org/licenses/by/2.0)], via Wikimedia Commons); P 52: Britannia & Co. (© Himani Verma), Berry pulao (© Himani Verma); P 53: Leopold Café (Snehal Jeevan Pailkar/Shutterstock.com); P 55: Dahi Handi celebrations in Mumbai (CRS PHOTO/Shutterstock.com), Mount Mary Church (arun sambhu mishra/Shutterstock.com); P 56: Gudi Padwa celebrations (Snehal Jeevan Pailkar/Shutterstock.com); P 57: Food stalls at Mohammad Ali Road (Pete Burana/Shutterstock.com); P 58: The Kala Ghoda Arts Festival (CRS PHOTO / Shutterstock.com); P 60: Chor Bazaar (Kalcutta/Shutterstock.com); P 61: Fisherwomen at the Sassoon Dock (CRS PHOTO/Shutterstock.com)

The views and opinions expressed in this book are the author's own and the facts are as reported by her, which have been verified to the extent possible, and the publishers are not in any way liable for the same.

The information in this book is based on research from bonafide sites and published books and is true to the best of the author's knowledge at the time of going to print. The author is not responsible for any further changes or developments occurring post the publication of this book. This series is not a comprehensive representation of the states of India but is intended to give children a flavour of the lifestyles and cultures of different states. All illustrations are artistic representations only.

ISBN 9780143445234

Design and layout by Quadrum Solutions Pvt. Ltd
Printed at Aarvee Promotions, India

Hello Kids!

I'm so happy you are reading this book. Did you know that India has some of the world's most colourful and action-packed cities?

I managed to visit many of them because my father was in the army and he was transferred to many places in India. And my brother and I followed him along with our mother, getting to live in a new place every few years. Even after I grew up, I was lucky to travel to many of India's cities.

Do you know the most amazing thing I discovered? I found that while some of India's cities are the most modern in the world, they also have the oldest histories. I tasted so many dishes that were invented in various cities. And I discovered that every city has its own unique and special feel.

So, if you, like me, like to know about different places, get set for some fun adventures in India's cities.

I do hope you enjoy these city adventures as much as I have enjoyed writing them. I would love to hear from you. So do write to me at sonia.mehta@quadrumltd.com.

Lots of love,
Sonia Aunty

Mishki and Pushka have come to visit Earth from their home planet, Zoomba. They have never seen such an amazing place. Zoomba doesn't have trees and mountains and rivers like Earth does. But the people look exactly the same. When they come to Earth, they meet a sweet old man whom they call Daadu Dolma. Daadu Dolma shows them all the wonderful places in India and tells Mishki and Pushka all about them.

Mishki and Pushka can't believe what they see. They have seen a lot of Earth, but they have never, ever seen a place like India.

They are off to explore India city by city ♫

Mishki

Mishki is a curious little girl. She is always asking loads of questions. On her home planet, she is always getting into trouble for poking her nose into things that are not her business.

Pushka

Pushka is Mishki's brother. He loves adventure. He is always ready for a new challenge. Whether it's climbing a mountain, or diving into a cold, cold sea, he is up for it.

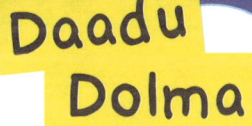

Daadu Dolma

Daadu Dolma is a wise old man who has lived on Earth longer than the mountains and the seas. No one knows quite how old he is, but he certainly has been around. He knows everything about everything.

Mishki and Pushka are visiting Mumbai with Daadu Dolma. They are so excited that they cannot sit still.

'I've heard that it's one of the biggest and busiest cities in the world,' exclaims Pushka.

'And I've heard that many film stars live in Mumbai,' adds Mishki, jumping up and down. 'And lots of other famous people too.'

'Both of you are right,' says Daadu, smiling. 'But that's not all. Mumbai also has a long and very interesting history.'

'Oh, wow! I love history,' Mishki says, clapping her hands in delight. 'Can we set off now?'

'Yes, let's go. Take your cameras and diaries along. There is lots to see and know about Mumbai,' Daadu tells them.

Mishki and Pushka grab their bags. They are

OFF TO MUMBAI!!!

A SNEAK PEEK

HELLO, MUMBAI!
Getting introduced to Mumbai
page 6

NATURE WALK
Enjoying nature in Mumbai
page 10

LONG, LONG AGO
A peek into Mumbai's history
page 14

STONE STORIES
Famous Mumbai monuments
page 18

NEIGHBOURHOODS
Unique neighbourhoods of Mumbai
page 28

TRANSPORT TALES
Mumbai's fascinating transport systems
page 34

LOCAL FOCAL
Mumbai's unique lifestyle and spirit
page 40

YUMMY MUMBAI!
Tasting typical Mumbai fare
page 46

GAME TIME
A fun Mumbai quiz
page 60

FESTIVAL FUN
Mumbai's festivals
page 54

DAADU'S DETECTIVE TRAIL

Pushka and Mishki are convinced that they are both great detectives and can crack any mystery or puzzle in the world.

Daadu has given them a puzzle to solve. But to solve it, they have to follow the trail of clues all through the book. Are you going to help them?

Here's what you have to do:

- Look for clues hidden in a little bag like this one.
- Each bag will have a letter of the alphabet in it.
- When you find a letter, write it down on page 61.
- When you have found all the letters, rearrange them to find the answer.

Get cracking and follow the trail of clues with Mishki and Pushka!

HELLO, MUMBAI!

What an amazing city? It seems to have it all—a fascinating history, incredible people and a special buzz all its own! I'd love to live here.

Right on the edge

The grand old city of Mumbai sits on the very edge of India's west coast. The waters of the Arabian Sea lap its shores. The city was perfect for the sea captains to bring in their ships. Even now, Mumbai has a massive port.

What's in a name?

For a long, long time, Mumbai was known as Bombay. There are two stories behind the name of this amazing city. At one time, Mumbai was occupied mainly by fisherfolk called *kolis*. Their patron goddess was called *Mumbadevi*. In the local language, that is Marathi, *aai* means mother. So the fisherfolk called their beloved city *Mumba Aai*—which became Mumbai when they said it fast. When the British came, they found it hard to pronounce Mumba Aai. So, they changed the city's name to Bombay.

MUMBAI MUMBAI
City of Dreams

Portuguese connection

According to another story, the Portuguese, who had landed in India centuries ago, thought this city had a lovely bay. In their language, they called it *Bom Bahia*, which meant beautiful bay.

Back to Mumbai

For many years after the British left, the city continued to be called Bombay. But some years ago, the local people felt that it was time to use the city's name in the local language. And so, the city's name was officially changed to Mumbai.

CLUE ALERT!

Seven islands

Many years ago in the Arabian Sea, there was an archipelago made up of seven tiny islands. A great many fisherfolk lived on these islands. These seven islands were known as Colaba, Mazagaon, Mahim, Parel, Isle of Bombay, Worli and Little Colaba (Old Woman's Island). Over time, these islands were joined together to make the great big metropolis of Mumbai.

Did you know?

The residents of Mumbai are locally known as Mumbaikars.

Mahim

Worli

Parel

Mazagaon

Isle of Bombay

Little Colaba

Colaba

Connected by bridges

Even after being joined, a large part of the Mumbai we know continued to be an island called Salsette that was connected to the mainland only by bridges. Imagine that!

Business boomer

The busy, bustling metropolis of Mumbai is India's business capital. Millions of people rush about, working hard to make their living. Some of India's most important banks, stock exchanges, business houses and news agencies are all based in Mumbai.

Oh, so crowded!

There are more than 20 million people living in Mumbai and more moving into the city every day. It is one of the most populated cities in the world. Scientists say that by the year 2020, nearly 28 million people will be living in Mumbai, making it the most crowded city in the world.

Did you know?

Mumbai has many slums where the poorest citizens live. But Mumbai also has the most number of billionaires in India. It ranks sixth in the world in terms of the number of billionaires it is home to. WOW!

NATURE WALK

Although Mumbai is a crowded city, it has its share of natural beauty too! Let's go for a nice walk and see some of Mumbai's green places.

Lakes galore

Mumbai has six lovely lakes that feed it water. They are the Vihar Lake, the Lower and Upper Vaitarna Lakes, the Tulsi Lake, the Tansa Lake and the Powai Lake. Every year, Mumbaikars wait with bated breath for these lakes to fill up with water during the rainy season. A good monsoon means that Mumbaikars have plenty of water through the year.

Mumbai monsoons are famous. Sometimes it rains so much that the streets are flooded and massive waves crash against the shore. Trains are late and schools are closed. But Mumbaikars love it all!

Powai lake

Park it!

Every city needs lungs made of green trees that help it breathe. Mumbai has a large national park called Sanjay Gandhi National Park. It's huge and is home to some fantastic and endangered wildlife. It's said that there are more than a 1000 types of plants, more than 250 breeds of migratory birds, and over fifty types of mammals. And wonder of wonders, more that 50,000 types of insects.

WOW! What a view!

Feathered visitors

Even though Mumbai is known as a concrete jungle because of its many skyscrapers, some rare wildlife occasionally visits the city. Did you know that a large population of flamingoes migrates to the swamps of Sewri and Bhandup every year?

Oh deer!

Going wild

There are leopards, sambar, barking deer, spotted deer and many other animals in Sanjay Gandhi National Park. There are crocodiles lurking in some of the lakes, so make sure you don't swim there. Some of the amazing birds you might get to see are jungle owlets, golden orioles, racket-tailed drongos, among others.

Flamingoes at Sewri, Mumbai

Hit the beach

Mumbai does have some lovely beaches. The coastline is dotted with creeks and bays. The most well known beaches are Madh, Marve, Girgaum and Juhu Chowpatty beaches.

CLUE ALERT!

Playing in the sand is so much fun!

Oshiwara river

River shiver

Three small rivers called the Dahisar River, the Poisar River and the Oshiwara River have their origins in Sanjay Gandhi National Park. A river called Mithi originates from Tulsi lake. Sadly, it is very polluted and it is quite a struggle to keep it clean.

Mangrove magic

Mumbai has large patches of land that are covered with mangroves. Mangroves are small shrub-like trees that grow particularly well in salty marshland. And that's exactly what Mumbai was at one time. A wonderful variety of wildlife lives in mangroves. Sadly, much of Mumbai's mangrove cover is being destroyed because of land being drained and reclaimed to build on.

RHYME AWAY

How many words can you think of that rhyme with **park**? At least ten?

_____   _____   _____   _____

_____   _____   _____   _____

LONG, LONG AGO

Although Mumbai is one of the world's most modern cities, it has a long and very interesting history. Let's jump right into its past.

Many rulers

At one time, the Mumbai region was under the rule of Emperor Ashoka. But one day, he decided he did not want to fight wars anymore. Instead, he became a peace-loving Buddhist. That's when these little islands were taken over by the Silhara dynasty, who ruled the kingdom of Gujarat. This dynasty ruled the area until the mid-1500s.

A gift for a princess

The Portuguese, who were great explorers, had set their sights on India and its riches. They grabbed the islands that make up Mumbai from the ruling king, Bahadur Shah of Gujarat. When the Portuguese princess, Catherine de Braganza married Charles II of England, the King of Portugal gave the islands to his daughter as a wedding gift.

Imagine getting a gift of islands!

Make way for the British

Some years later, it was the British who decided they would rule India. They defeated king after king, and took over territories. Soon India was a British colony, ruled by the East India Company. The British found the islands a perfect place to make their headquarters. So they moved their headquarters from Surat in Gujarat to these islands. This was when Bombay, as we know it, was formed.

The East India Company headquarters in Surat

SHIP SHAPE

The Portuguese arrived on ships like these. Can you spot ten differences between these two ships?

Connected to the world

Events were unfolding in the world even as the British were busy settling into India. The Suez Canal opened up a new route for ships travelling from west to east and suddenly, trade with India began to boom. This made Bombay one of India's largest and most important ports.

Building more and more

The British were thorough in their planning. First, they merged the seven islands into a single mass. They began many projects. They built pipelines, roads, bridges and railways. The first railway was built between a station called Bori Bunder and Thane (a suburb of present-day Mumbai). In April 1853, the first train chugged its way across Bombay.

CLUE ALERT!

Fighting for independence

The people of India were fed up with having the British lay down laws that were often unfair to Indians. There were riots across the country, as people demanded that the British leave India. And finally, in 1947, the British left and India became a free country.

The city takes part

Bombay played an important role in the freedom struggle. A lot of action took place in Bombay, and many of these historical places are still there for us to see.

FREEDOM

The Royal Indian Navy staged a fierce mutiny at the Bombay Harbour.

The Indian National Congress was formed at the Gokuldas Tejpal Sanskrit Pathshala, a place you can visit even now.

The Quit India Movement was started in Bombay, at the Gowalia Tank Maidan (now called the August Kranti Maidan).

Members of the Congress met secretly to formulate strategies against the British in a building called Congress House.

Mahatma Gandhi lived in Bombay, at a place called Mani Bhavan, from where he orchestrated his silent protests.

STONE STORIES

How cool! Mumbai has awesome skyscrapers right next to some really old buildings. Isn't that amazing? I can't wait to see them all.

Grand welcome for a king and queen

King George V of England and his wife Queen Mary decided to visit India. In those days, they had to travel by ship and the journey took nearly a month. To welcome their royal majesties, the officials decided to build the grand Gateway of India in 1919. It took four years to build. Now the Gateway of India is a major tourist attraction.

An arrow and a river

Banganga means the arrow of the river Ganga. Banganga is an ancient water tank with a temple next to it at a place called Walkeshwar. Tucked away in the midst of modern skyscrapers, this temple-tank makes you feel you have travelled back in time. It has a lovely story too! People say when Rama was on his way to Sri Lanka to rescue Sita from the demon, Ravana, he stopped here for a brief rest. He shot an arrow into the ground, and water burst forth.

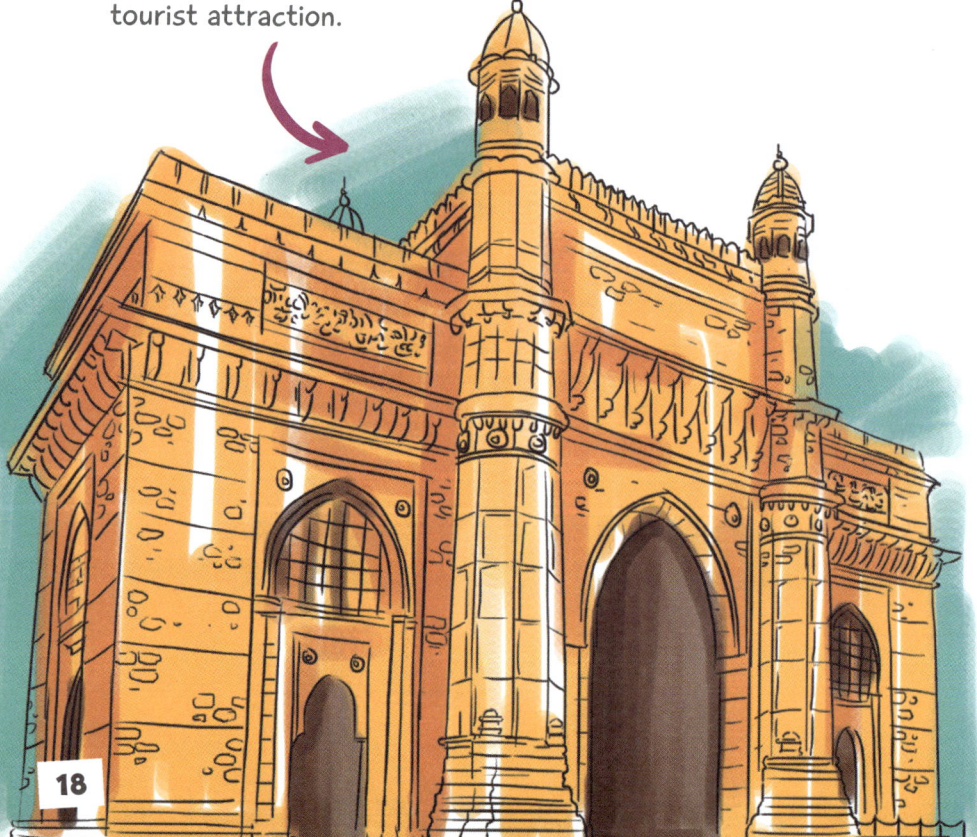

Wash, wash, wash away!

Imagine rows and rows of open-air wash pens, each with its own flogging stone. Now imagine hundreds of washermen washing tons of clothes every day. Dhobi Ghat (meaning the washerman's steps) is over a hundred years old. All day, more than 7000 washermen wash, bleach and scrub garments sent to them by nearby laundries, hotels and clubs. They dry them on clotheslines, iron them neatly and send them back.

Dhobi Ghat has been mentioned in the *Guinness Book of World Records* too!

A station to remember

When you first see Victoria Terminus, you might think it's a royal palace. But Mumbaikars know it as one of the world's busiest train stations. It's more than a hundred years old and most of Mumbai's out-of-town trains arrive and depart from here. It was named after Queen Victoria to commemorate her golden jubilee year. Now it has been renamed Chhatrapati Shivaji Maharaj Terminus.

It has eighteen platforms at which trains arrive and leave. That's a lot of platforms for a single station.

Mount Mary Basilica Church, Bandra

A church on a hill

The Mount Mary Basilica on a little hill in the charming suburb of Bandra is more than a century old. People say that the statue of Jesus was brought here by Jesuits, all the way from Portugal in the sixteenth century BCE. Followers have so much faith in this church, that they believe that any wish they pray for here will be fulfilled.

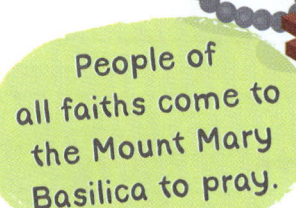

People of all faiths come to the Mount Mary Basilica to pray.

Over 400 years old

St Andrew's Church is said to be more than four centuries old. It was built when Bombay was under Portuguese control. You wouldn't believe how old this church is because it's now surrounded by chic restaurants and shops. But it's a strong old structure all right. It has stood strong against invasions by different armies over the years.

Living on a prayer

An architect was once asked to build a building near the sea. But the wall that was supposed to keep the sea out kept collapsing. The architect had a dream. He dreamt that there was a statue of a goddess buried deep underground in that very spot. He decided to check if there was any truth to his dream. To his amazement, an idol of a goddess was indeed found there. A magnificent temple was built on that spot. This is the famous Mahalaxmi Temple in Mumbai.

A tomb in the middle of the sea

The Haji Ali Dargah in Mumbai is an amazing sight. It is right in the middle of the sea. It is the tomb where Haji Ali, a Muslim saint, is buried. People from all over the world come to pray here. They have to cross a narrow path on the sea to reach this amazing mosque. When it is high tide, the path is completely under water. It can only be reached only during low tide.

CLUE ALERT!

Old, old, old caves

Nearly twenty centuries ago, some Buddhist monks went in search of a calm place in which to meditate. They found the perfect spot in a mountainside, made of basalt rock. They carved out deep caves in which they sat and meditated. Over the centuries, more Buddhists came and added to the caves. The Kanheri Caves, in Mumbai's suburbs, are a set of one hundred caves full of Buddhist carvings, art and sculptures.

Amazing!

Ding dong bell 🔔

High above a majestic building is a stunning clock tower called the Rajabai Tower. You'd never believe that the magnificent building it crowns, is the old Mumbai University building. It was inspired by the famous Big Ben in London and it sure looks like it. Not only does it have elaborate arches and details in a Venetian-Gothic style, it also has a porch for horse-drawn carriages to drive up to.

Rajabai Tower was funded by a man called Roychand Premchand. The story goes that his mother, who was blind, got her cue to have dinner when she heard this clock chime.

To market, to market

Crawford Market (now officially called Mahatma Jyotiba Phule Mandai) is a busy, busy place with stalls piled with fruit, vegetables, poultry and a whole lot of wholesale goods. The amazing thing about this market is its architecture. There are friezes and columns and a wonderful skylight to let the light in. The market is more than a hundred years old.

Crawford Market was the first market in India to get electricity in 1882.
WOW!

The Kipling Bungalow

Did you know that Rudyard Kipling, the author of *The Jungle Book* was born in Mumbai? His father was an architect and was the first ever principal of the now famous J.J. Institute of Applied Art. The house that Kipling was born in is still there for us to visit. It's a pretty bluish-green bungalow sitting right in the middle of the J.J. Campus.

23

A circle and a square

The Flora Fountain statue is a gorgeous sculpture of a Roman goddess called Flora set in the middle of a lovely old fountain. It's in the heart of Mumbai's oldest business district. There are five roads leading off it. People call it Mumbai's Picadilly. A lovely monument was later built here to honour the martyrs who fought for Maharashtra's freedom. Now the square is called Hutatma Chowk or Martyrs' Square.

A treasure house of knowledge

A learned group of people once met in Bombay and decided to build a library where 'useful knowledge could be stored'. And so the Literary Society of Bombay was formed, and a wonderful building was built. This building is now known as the Asiatic Society of Mumbai. It looks like a Greek or Roman building. Inside is a treasure of knowledge.

At one time, an old fort stood in this area, with three gates. The Church Gate (which is now a famous station), the Bazaar Gate and the Apollo Gate. The whole area is still known as Fort by Mumbaikars.

The Asiatic Society has more than 100,000 rare books. Over 3000 of these are in Persian. It even has nearly 12,000 rare coins.

Dock lock

Because Mumbai is a port city, it has a lot of docks all around, used for different things. The Sassoon Docks are one of the oldest. They are home to one of Mumbai's largest and busiest fish markets. Once, there was only sea here. A man called David Sassoon, who was one of Mumbai's first famous Jews, reclaimed the land. Ships began to land here to trade cotton, something that the old Bombay was famous for.

Fresh FISH

MATCH IT

Match the two columns to get the correct names of these famous places in Mumbai.

Sassoon	Hutatma	Church	Crawford	Flora

Market	Fountain	Gate	Docks	Chowk

A bridge to remember

The Bandra–Worli Sea Link is a modern masterpiece and tourists come and gape at it in awe. It's said that the cement and steel used in the bridge equals the girth of the earth. Oh, wow!

The official name for this bridge is Rajiv Gandhi Sea Link.

←Elephanta Caves

These beautiful cave temples are just a quick boat ride away from the Gateway of India. The most amazing structure here is the Shiva Temple. There are many stories about the carvings in these caves. Some say a great warrior prince called Pulakesin II ordered these carvings to celebrate a victory. Some others say that soldiers of ancient armies did their target practice in these caves, using them to keep enemies away.

Gandhiji's Home

For many years, during India's fight for independence, Mahatma Gandhi lived in Mumbai in a house on this quiet, leafy lane. The name of his house was Mani Bhavan. So many years later, the charming house still stands and is now a museum filled with books, pictures and montages of his eventful life.

NEIGHBOURHOODS

No two Mumbai neighbourhoods are alike. Busy, overcrowded markets; leafy lanes; beaches, office areas, fish markets and shopping zones abound. Let's take a look at some unique neighbourhoods.

Plum slum

Dharavi, one of Asia's largest slums is in Mumbai. It's a miracle of living. More than three lakh people live in Dharavi. Along with other slums, it is estimated that more than half of Mumbai's population lives in slums. Amazingly, these slums are busy, productive places. Tourists visit Dharavi and come away amazed.

CLUE ALERT!

Mumbai's slums have a terrific community life.

A little bit of London

Walk down the streets of Ballard Estate, and you could well be in an old part of London. This is a lovely business district full of lovely old buildings, designed in the European Renaissance style. But guess what! At one time, this whole area was a port and before that, it was sea. The land was reclaimed years ago.

Ballard Estate is named after Colonel J.A. Ballard. He founded the Bombay Port Trust, an organisation that oversaw the trading activities that went on in Bombay's ports.

A ladder so far

One of Bombay's first suburbs (though now it's considered central to the city) is a neighbourhood called Dadar. The Portuguese built a lot of buildings and churches here. Later, it became the hub of Marathi culture. Even now, you'll find a glorious mix of churches, temples, markets and a busy, busy railway station in Dadar.

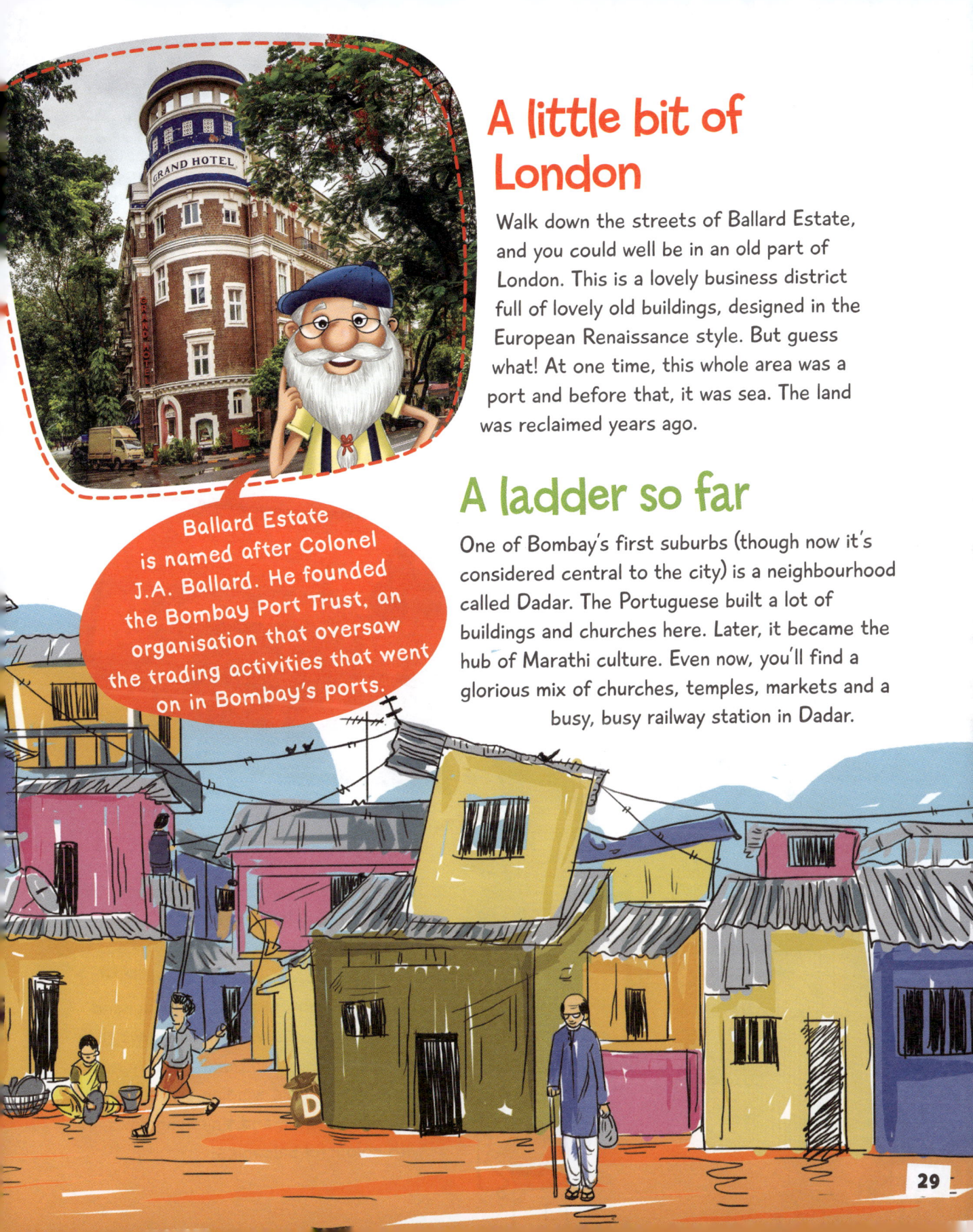

Simply charming!

Bandra, a charming neighbourhood in the heart of Mumbai, has a culture all its own. In the fifteenth century BCE, the Portuguese fell in love with this area. They began to build churches, streets and houses here. He burnt the little fishing town and began to build churches, streets and houses. Over the years, the area changed hands from the Portuguese, to Islamic rulers, to the British and finally to independent India. Now it is home to many famous movie stars.

One of seven islands

A tiny island that has become a bustling suburb is the area called Mahim. At one time, it was called Mahikawati. When the island was captured by Islamic rulers from the rulers of Gujarat, they built a famous mosque and a shrine here. Even later, when the British captured it, they built the Mahim fort to protect themselves from the Portuguese. All these spots are still there for us to visit. Now, Mahim is part of the mainland because it is connected by land reclaimed from the sea.

The Mahim Fort

Right out of Goa

In the heart of a busy, bustling part of the city lies a little piece of land that makes you feel you are in Goa or even perhaps Portugal. Called Khotachi Wadi (after Mr Khot, the man who founded it), this little village has bungalows that are built in the traditional Portuguese style. It has little winding streets, a charming chapel, and tiny bungalows with colourful balconies.

The thieves' market

Chor Bazaar literally means the Thieves' Market. Legend goes that thieves would sell their stolen wares at this crazy market that is almost 150 years old. You find old tyres, furniture, lamps, doors, ancient toys, photo frames, antique mirrors . . . just about anything you can think of.

The story goes that this market got its name when some items stolen from Queen Victoria, were found here.

HIDDEN WORDS

Mahikawati. A big word all right. Can you make ten words from it?

MAHIKAWATI

_____ _____ _____ _____

_____ _____ _____ _____

_____

The Queen's Necklace

When the islands that make up Mumbai were joined, a lot of land was reclaimed from the sea. In the south of Bombay, this land made a perfect crescent shape. This was where a promenade called Marine Drive was built. Lovely buildings were constructed in a style called Art Deco. Street lamps lit up the long, three-kilometre stretch. When it's seen at night, it looks like the necklace of a queen. And that's why Marine Drive is also called Queen's Necklace.

Colaba Causeway

Colaba, as we saw earlier, was one of the islands that made up Bombay. Many ships would dock here and it soon became overcrowded. The British ordered a causeway to be built to handle the crowds. Over time, the island of Colaba was joined to the main island. Now, Colaba Causeway (renamed Shahid Bhagat Singh Marg) is a shopper's dream. It's full of cafés, art galleries, street shops and tiny boutiques.

Marine Drive is historic. It has said that the famous actor, Amitabh Bachchan, slept on its benches when he was a young out-of-work actor. It has also been featured in many movies.

Just beachy

Mumbai has many beaches. But perhaps two of the most famous beaches are Girgaum and Juhu Chowpatty. People flock to these beaches to enjoy the sand and sun and to eat some of Mumbai's most amazing street food. There are vendors selling balloons, toys, roasted peanuts and the ever popular chaat—a typical Mumbai street snack.

Cricketers are born

Every Sunday, in a large open space called Shivaji Park, you'll see lots of young children, dressed in cricketing whites, playing a serious game of cricket. Shivaji Park is where, Mumbaikars proudly claim, great cricketers are discovered. Sachin Tendulkar, Sunil Gavaskar and Ravi Shastri are just some who played here when they were boys, and who went on to become world famous.

TRANSPORT TALES

Mumbai's transport systems are like a miracle, when you think about how many people use them every day. Trains and buses ply in the city almost twenty four hours a day. Mumbaikars never seem to rest!

Train tango

Mumbai local trains are among the busiest in the world. They carry more than two billion passengers in their coaches every year.

Track record

Each day, about 200 local trains make more than 2000 trips on nearly 300 kilometres of railway track. These busy trains carry more commuters per mile than any railway in the world.

Filled to bursting

Although the trains were originally built to fit 1700 people, more than thrice that number squeeze in. Can you imagine the crowd? This is called a Super Dense Crush Load.

WHEW!!!

More than seven million people travel on Mumbai trains every day. That's almost as much as the population of Israel.

OMG!

Ladies Special

To keep women from being crushed, Mumbai trains are among the few in the world to have separate compartments only for women.

Control point

You can imagine how busy the railways' Central Traffic Control Room is. There is an electronic map that covers an entire wall and the movement of every single train is tracked. During peak hours, more than 400 trains move on just four tracks. So you can imagine what could happen to the others if even one train is delayed. It's a miracle that it all works!

Bus boom!

Mumbai was the first city in India to have a local bus service. In 1926, the first public bus was driven from Afghan Church to Crawford Market, both of which are now important heritage spots.

Here comes the big red bus

The familiar red buses that ply the busy streets of Mumbai are called BEST buses. Not because they're the best, but because BEST stands for Brihanmumbai Electric Supply and Transport. At one time, these buses were actually tramways, and the original name was the Bombay Tramway Company.

CLUE ALERT!

Busy wheels

Now the BEST runs more than 3500 buses. These buses have nearly 400 routes and carry more than 4.5 million passengers every day. More than 3500 people work to make this happen.

A museum of buses

A simple man called P.D. Paranjpe, who was a BEST officer, began to collect bus tickets and old ticket issuing machines. Soon, he had so many, that he started a museum. Now you can learn about the BEST's history, see models of its buses and all sorts of fun things at the BEST Transport Museum at the Anik Bus Depot near Chembur.

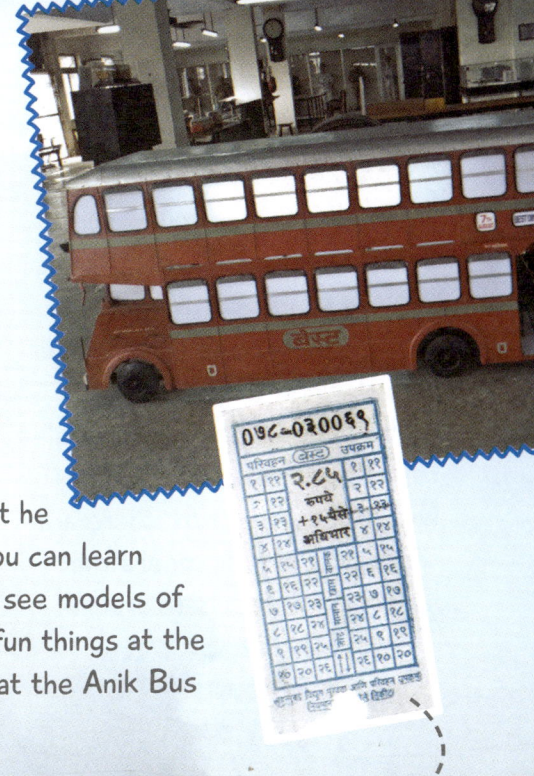

Ticket to ride!

BUS FUSS

Which two buses are exactly alike?

A

B

C

D

E

F

Kaali-peeli

Kaali-peeli means yellow and black. That's what the taxis that dot the streets of Mumbai are called. These taxis hit the roads in 1911, when they began to replace the horse-drawn buggies called Victorias (named after Queen Victoria). Now there are thousands of kaali-peelis that help ferry passengers around.

Thanks to new car services that private companies run, the number of kaali-peeli taxis is decreasing. This is sad, because these cheerful cabs are what Mumbai is known for.

Smaller cousins

The auto-rickshaw (simply called auto by Mumbaikars in a hurry) is a smaller cousin of the taxi. This three-wheeler—also yellow and black—can fit just two people. It can perform miracles on the roads by turning a full 360 degrees on the spot. Because of traffic congestion, autos are not allowed in certain parts of Mumbai.

Busy busy airport

The Mumbai airport is a busy place, all right. Its new terminal is said to be among the best in the world. It covers more than 1400 acres and it has granite enough to cover twenty-seven football fields.

The Mumbai airport handles more than 900 take-offs and landings every day—among the highest in the world. Gosh! Can you imagine the control room?

WHOA!

WHAT'S ODD?

Can you find the odd word in each row?

1 taxi   bus   train   rickshaw   car

2 airport   dock   football field   terminal   runway

3 tracks   compartments   engine   coaches   chimney

LOCAL FOCAL

There's something about Mumbai, that's just so . . . Mumbai! The smells, the sights, the sounds . . . Mumbai is definitely quite unique. Let's discover what makes the spirit of Mumbai.

Living together

One of the most unique systems of Mumbai is the chawl system. It's been around for over a hundred years. Chawls are large residential buildings with tiny apartments, all connected by a long common balcony that runs the length of the building. Life in a chawl is unique. People share space, bathrooms, problems, festivals and life.

Mill till

At one time, Mumbai was the hub of the textile industry. It had more than 130 textile mills. Many businessmen made their fortune in textiles. Thousands of people worked in these mills, and a unique culture developed. But slowly, the textile industry died out and the mills began to shut down. Some were turned into fashionable shops and restaurants; while some are in ruins, covered with slippery moss. But they are a part of Mumbai's landscape.

WHOA!

Tiffin time

The *dabbawalas* of Mumbai are famous all over the world. Guess what their job is? Carrying lunch boxes from peoples' homes to their offices, so that people can get a nice, hot meal. The dabbawalas are famous because of their complicated system that works like a relay race. One dabbawala picks up the lunch box from a house, he then passes it on to the next, who passes it on and this goes on till it reaches the person it is meant for.

More than 5000 dabbawalas deliver over 200,000 custom made lunches across Mumbai city.

Did you know that the dabbawala system has been recognised as one of the best-managed systems by an international business magazine called Forbes?

41

Money, money, money

Many say that money makes Mumbai go round. That's probably true because it is the financial capital of India. Thousands of people are busy making money on the Bombay Stock Exchange. Years ago, all the stock brokers used to sit under a banyan tree and conduct their business. As the number of brokers increased, they began to look for a permanent place to work from. A wealthy businessman called Premchand Roychand built a building on a street that came to be known as Dalal Street (it means brokers' street).

Now, the Bombay Stock Exchange is a magnificent, modern building, where millions of rupees are earned (and sometimes lost).

Cricket Crazy

The people of India are crazy about cricket. And Mumbaikars are right up there. Most cities have just one, but Mumbai has three massive cricket stadia where international matches are held. One of them, the most historic, is the Brabourne Stadium.

Brabourne Stadium is historic for many reasons.

It was India's first proper sporting venue.

The first T-20 match was played here, between India and Australia.

It was here that Sachin Tendulkar scored his first double century in first class cricket, helping India defeat Australia.

The Parsis of Mumbai

Some centuries ago, a group of Zoroastrians fled from Iran to escape persecution. They landed in Gujarat. When the British began developing Bombay as a commercial hub, many Parsis migrated here. They built businesses that grew to become some of India's largest. They set up research institutes, built theatres, and introduced Mumbai to a lifestyle quite their own. Today, the Parsi colonies where many of them live are tiny hubs, inside which life is quite different from the rest of Mumbai.

Jamsetji Tata—who built the Tata empire; Homi Bhabha, the scientist after whom the Bhabha Atomic research Centre was named; Ardeshir Godrej, who built the Godrej group of companies; these are just some famous Parsis.

A-fishing we will go

Mumbai, as we know now, was once just a little fishing village. Its earliest residents, the *kolis*, still live in pockets that are tiny fishing communities called *koliwadas*. They take their little boats out to sea every morning and sell their catch at the local fish markets. They have many songs and customs that are all about the sea.

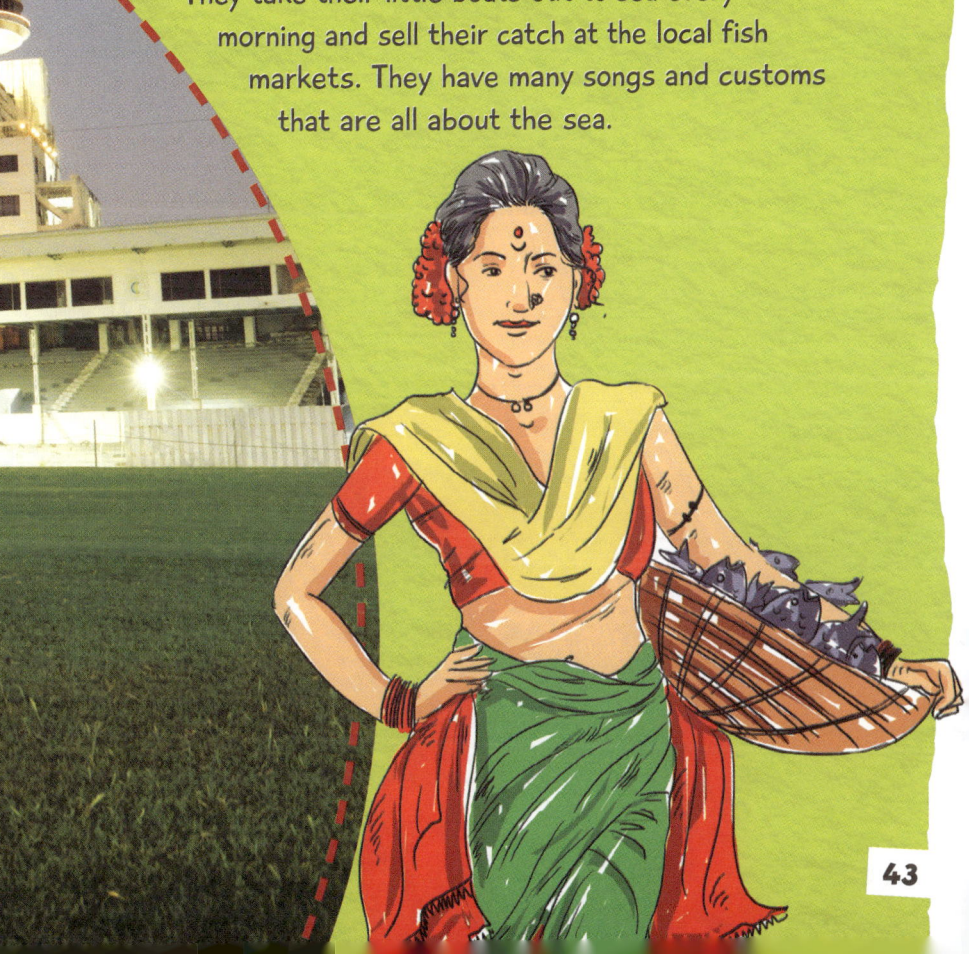

43

Bollywood boom

When people think of Mumbai, they think of Bollywood. Mumbai is the heart of the Hindi film industry. India's oldest studios are right here. Filmistan, Mehboob Studios, Bombay Talkies, RK Studios . . . these were the studios where great classics were shot.

R.K. Studios, Chembur, Mumbai

First Indian Film ever shot

A film-maker called Dadasaheb Phalke made India's first ever film and, naturally, it was shot in Mumbai, in the neighbourhood of Dadar. That first step was the beginning of Bollywood, one of the world's largest film industries.

Bollywood is a mix of two words—Bombay and Hollywood. Although people from the film industry don't particularly like to use that word. They like to simply call it the Hindi Film Industry.

The city of dreams

Mumbai is called the City of Dreams because every year, millions of young people flock to Mumbai hoping to make their dream of becoming famous in Mumbai's film industry come true.

Home of the stars

World-famous actors have made their home in Mumbai for over a hundred years. All the famous Hindi filmstars live in Mumbai. Amitabh Bachchan's house always has a huge crowd of fans waiting outside, hoping to catch a glimpse of their idol. It's said that he comes out once in a while to greet his fans. *Mannat*, Shah Rukh Khan's home, is always surrounded by fans trying to take a selfie with his house in the background. Oh, it's a star-studded place all right!

Lights! Camera! Action!

A whole lot of films in Mumbai are shot in a place called Dadasaheb Phalke Film City—a massive studio that was built specifically for shooting films. It has temples, jails, police stations, palaces, bungalows, helipads and all sorts of locations that people might need as a setting for their movie. Sounds exciting!

Did you know that there are special Film City tours that show visitors how a movie is made inside Film City?

JUMBLE TUMBLE

Pushka loves all the things that Mumbaikars love. He's trying to figure out the answers to this quiz. Can you?

1. Mumbaikars are really crazy about trckice _____

2. A lot of people in Mumbai live in whcasl _____

3. ilmf _____ City is a place that has all kinds of ready sets for movies.

4. aalld _____ street is a street where stock brokers do their business.

YUMMY MUMBAI

I've heard so much about Mumbai's street food. I'm going to taste it all. Let's get started!

FOODIE STREETS

Mumbai is dotted with *khao gallis* (literally meaning food streets) that are packed with street vendors. Food carts are piled high with all sorts of goodies. All these are typical Mumbai fare.

Vada Pav

This is a yummy potato dumpling, squashed inside a pav (bread) and eaten with chillies and spicy chutneys. This snack was something mill workers would grab on their back from a late-night shift. Now everyone gobbles them up. That's how good they taste.

पाटील वड़ापाव

Bhel Puri

Everyone has heard of this amazing snack. Puffed rice with onions, potatoes, sweet and spicy chutneys, and found on many street corners—this is said to be a Mumbai invention.

Misal Pav

This is another Mumbai treat. It is a mix of sprouts served in a spicy curry and eaten with pav.

FOODOKU

Try and solve this sudoku. Make sure that every fruit is there in every row and column, once.

The Bombay Sandwich

Who would have thought a simple sandwich could taste so good? But the street corners of Mumbai are peppered with tiny sandwich stands at which vendors make amazing tomato, cucumber and potato sandwiches. The man who started it must have been called Raju, because many of these sandwich stalls are called Raju Sandwich stalls.

MUST TRY!

Zunka Bhakri

Simple farmer's fare, this is yummy dish made of a spicy, gooey paste that tastes better than it looks. People eat it along with healthy rotis made of jowar.

Kutchi Dabeli

Dabeli means pressed. Kutchi tells us it came originally from Kutch, in Gujarat. But now this dish inhabits the streets of Mumbai. It's a delicious potato mash, pressed hard into the ever-popular pav.

Koliwada fish

Since Mumbai is a land of fisherfolk, obviously the fish here is amazing. The fishing community (kolis) have a special way of cooking their fish, that's called koliwada fish. It's spicy, crisp and mouth-wateringly perfect.

CLUE ALERT!

CHAI TIME

This tea-seller is dispensing chai to people. Can you spot ten differences between the two pictures?

THE FOLK BEHIND THE FOOD

There are some genius cooks who have become icons and made their mark on the city's food scene. Let's meet some of them.

Sardar's

A young man called Sardar Ahmed sold fruit to hungry mill workers outside the mill gates. He decided to make a dish that was nutritious, tasty and affordable too. And that's how he invented the pav bhaaji. His shop, called Sardar's, in Tardeo, serves up the best pav bhaaji in Mumbai.

Muchhad Paanwala

This moustache has to be seen to be believed. Sitting in a tiny little paan (betel leaf) shop in Kemps Corner, a man with a magnificent moustache dispenses paan of all kinds. He's called Muchhad (meaning man with a moustache). It's a simple shop but all the rich and famous people make sure they get their paan from him.

Mucchad has many fans. They've got together and created a website for him. *Just imagine.*

Yummmmy!

Frankies

Many years ago, a Sikh gentleman called Amarjit Singh Tibb tasted a Lebanese dish he loved. He thought he could create a similar dish, one that Indian people would like. And so he created what is now known as the Frankie. His wife, Surinder Tibb cooked and kneaded and together they came up with an amazing snack made of rotis stuffed with curried meats called Frankies.

Bademiya

There was once a young boy named Mohammed Yaseen who worked in a butcher's shop. He wanted to start his own cart to serve kebabs to hungry naval officers who worked at the port. With just ₹20, he started his cart. He became so popular that his little cart grew and grew. As he grew older, his sons and grandsons joined him. Soon, the cart he started, called Bademiya, became so popular, that all the rich and famous began to stop there for a late night bite.

Now Bademiya has its own restaurants. What a journey for a simple lad.

ODD ONE OUT

There's an odd word in every row. Can you circle it?

roti	bread	toast	biscuit	spinach
potato	carrot	cucumber	radish	ginger
restaurant	café	diner	grocer	coffee shop
apple	orange	kiwi	tomato	cabbage
cashew	almond	pea	macadamia	chestnut

Apart from the amazing street food of Mumbai, there are some historical eateries that have been around for years and years. Let's visit some.

Mama Kane

Over a century ago, a man called Narayan Vishnu Kane shut down his traditional business of making Ganesha idols and moved to Bombay. He decided to serve Maharashtrian vegetarian food to daily labourers. His family got to work cooking in their home kitchen. Now Mama Kane, as his little eatery is called, is one of Mumbai's best-known restaurants for traditional Maharashtrian food.

It's like eating at home. No wonder the restaurant is always packed.

Britannia

Almost a hundred years ago, a man named Rashid Kohinoor decided to move to Bombay and start a café called Café Britannia, to serve Parsi food. He had no idea that his little café would become one of Bombay's best-known restaurants, with people stopping by from all over the world. His sons and his grandsons kept his dream alive, and even now, in the leafy lanes of Ballard Estate, this little café serves its loyal customers.

You will simply love the berry pulao here.

yum

Leopold Café

The year was 1871, when an Iranian man ran a store that sold cooking oil. One day, he began cooking food and selling it at his store. And soon, his food became so popular, that he turned into a café. And so Leopold Café was born in Colaba. Today it is very, very popular with locals and foreigners as well. It's always packed!

You might have to wait for a table!

From Iran with love

If you go around the older parts of Mumbai, you will see very old, charming little cafés. These are the famous Irani restaurants. When the Zoroastrian community from Persia (modern-day Iran) made their home in India, many settled in Mumbai. They set up these lovely cafés, where people could drop in for a chat and drink the famous Irani chai.

Bhagat Tarachand

Many years ago, a man called Tarachand Chawla started a small eatery serving yummy vegetarian food in Lahore (now in Pakistan). But when India became independent, and was divided into two nations, Tarachand left Lahore and came to Mumbai. He continued his business and now, more than 115 years later, his sons and grandsons have expanded it. People come from all over the country to eat the delicious food that is a mix of Sind and Punjab.

I've tasted the yummy khari biscuit and bun maska at an Irani café. They are specialties.

Sadly, these restaurants are becoming rarer. Now there are just about twenty-five.

FESTIVAL FUN

Mumbai is famous for some festivals. Many of these are public celebrations, where people get together and make merry on the streets in keeping with the Mumbai spirit. Anything for a good time!

Go Ganpati

Ganpati or Ganesha is the beloved elephant-headed Hindu god. His birthday, Ganesh Chaturthi, is celebrated in Mumbai in the biggest and most dramatic fashion. Mud or clay idols of Ganesha are brought home. The idols range in size from tiny to as tall as a five-storey building. After praying to Ganesha for ten days, people take the idols to the sea or a river to immerse them.

GANPATI BAPPA MORYA!

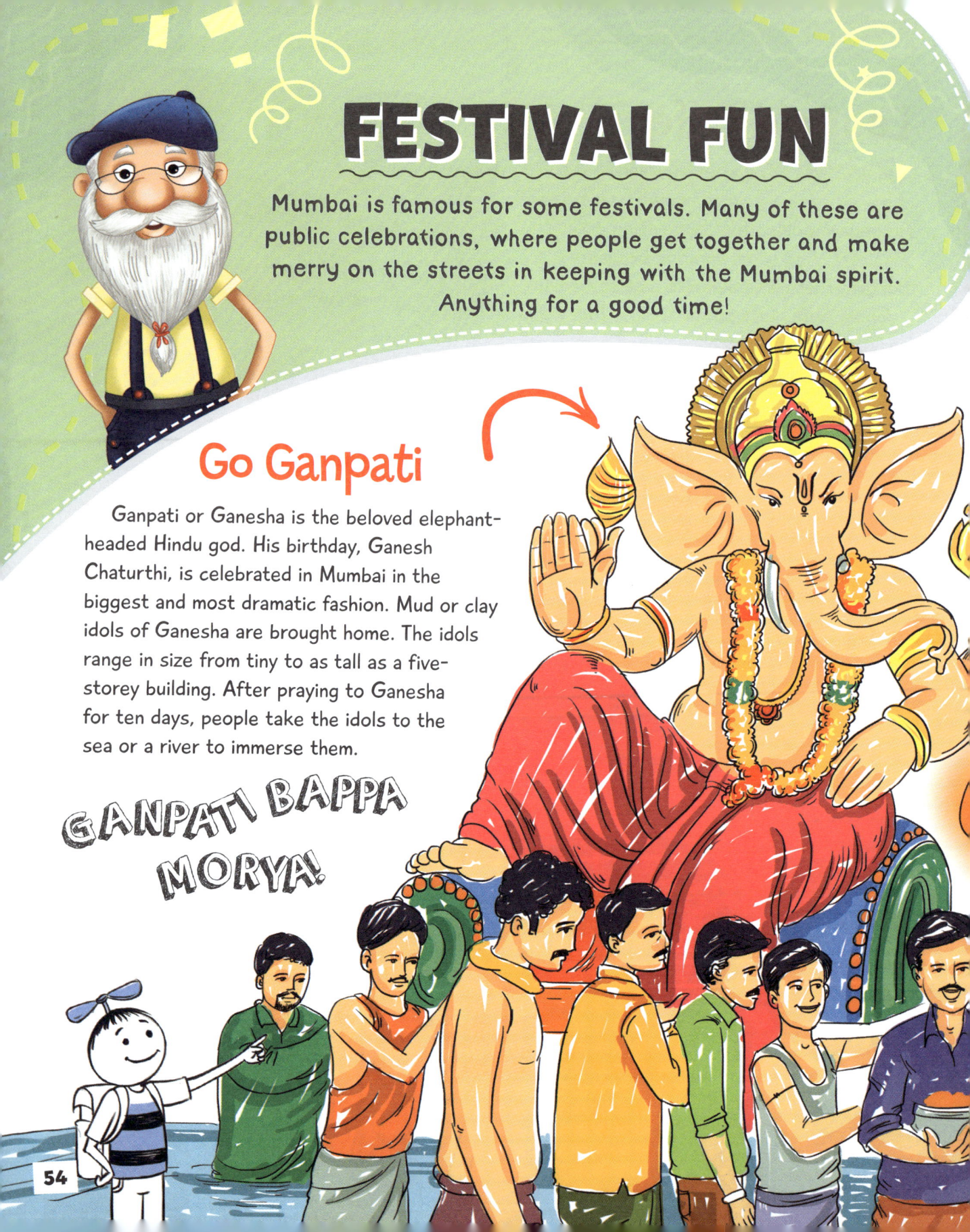

Govinda ala re ala

Janmashtami is the day Hindus believe the god Krishna was born. Krishna loved ghee and butter. As a child, he would climb up on the shoulders of his friends to get at the butter his mother put out of his reach. To celebrate his birth, people hang a mud pot full of goodies two or three storeys high. Then people form a huge human pyramid, and one intrepid youth tries to climb to the top to break the pot. Then everyone shares the goodies. All the while, people sing 'Govinda Ala Re Ala'.

Govinda is another name for Krishna.

Fun, food, fiesta and faith

Every September, for one week, the little suburb of Bandra goes crazy as millions of people flock to Mount Mary Church to pray. Over the years, this has turned into one of Mumbai's largest fairs. There are food stalls, clothes, trinkets and a whole lot of fun and excitement surrounding this fair.

Honouring a great man

On 6 December, each year, lakhs of people from all over the country get on to trains and buses and gather at Shivaji Park in Mumbai. They collect to honour the memory of Dr B.R. Ambedkar, a social reformer, who did a lot for Dalits. They stand for hours in a long line to visit his memorial, Chaitya Bhoomi.

A coconut day

Nariyal Poornima is a day that fisherfolk celebrate, to mark the end of the rains. This is when they can take their boats out to sea again, after a long break. They paint their fishing boats in bright colours, and light tiny oil lamps that they float amidst the waves. Then they break a coconut against the prow of the boat and off they go, to catch fish.

They're happy to go to sea again.

The biggest clue: Rearrange all the letters you've found and make the word on page 61. **Hint:** They are unique to Mumbai and keep people from getting hungry.

Oh, Gudi! It's time to celebrate

Gudi Padva, the Maharashtrian new year, marks the beginning of the new year according to the Hindu calendar, which is quite different from the Roman calendar that we usually follow. People decorate their houses and cook yummy feasts. Then they put up the *gudi*. This is a bamboo stick, topped with a small decorated vessel. It's propped up on verandahs, windows or balconies, and is meant to keep evil away and bring good luck.

There are fun parades during which people do the famous lezim dance.

A festival of togetherness

Eid-ul-Fitr is a festival that is celebrated with great enthusiasm in Mumbai. On this day, people of the Muslim faith gather in huge numbers at Azad Maidan (one of Mumbai's largest public grounds) and pray together. Mosques everywhere are gaily decorated. After prayer, people go to a street called Mohammed Ali Road to eat yummy dishes made specially on Eid. This is the day the month-long fasting of Ramzan comes to an end.

A new year for Parsis

Pateti, or Parsi New Year, is celebrated with aplomb by the Parsis in Mumbai. This is the day, it's said, on which the Zoroastrian community first landed in India when they migrated from Persia (modern-day Iran).

So much to celebrate!

TWIN GUDIS

Look at these gudis, cheerfully fluttering away. Can you find two that are exactly alike?

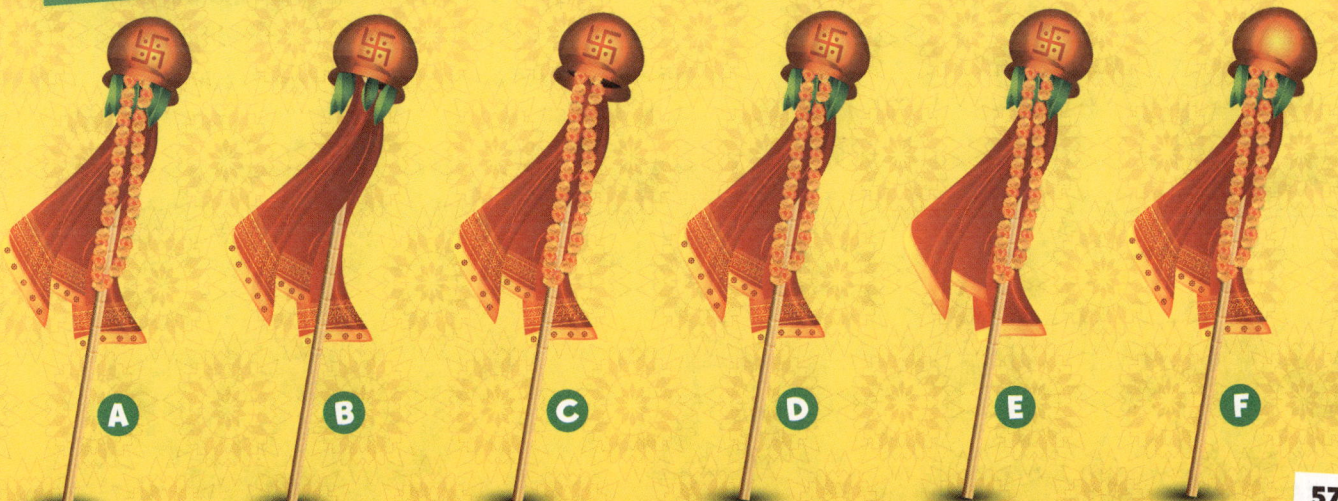

A   B   C   D   E   F

CULTURE CRAZE

Not all of Mumbai's fairs and festivals are religious. There are many fun cultural events that people thoroughly enjoy as well.

Food, fun and art

The Kala Ghoda (means black horse) Festival is held in February every year, during which thousands collect to enjoy art and culture. There are street plays, things to buy, food to eat, dance performances, sculptures and art installations. The atmosphere is full of excitement as artists from around India come together and showcase their talent and their wares.

Mumbai Marathon

Thousands of feet pound the street as Mumbaikars take to running or walking on the emptied roads of Mumbai. The Mumbai Marathon is now an event that is much looked forward to. Every January, the old and young, men and women, children and adults, all come out in full force to support different charities.

Run for a cause!

Mood Indigo

IIT (the Indian Institute of Technology) is a famous college of engineering. Many years ago, a group of students began a music and cultural festival. They called it Mood Indigo. There were local rock bands, classical musicians and pop groups that came together. There were bonfires, singing and dancing all night long. Now Mood Indigo is one of Asia's largest college festivals.

The IITians who started this fest were big fans of the singer Frank Sinatra. He had a song called 'Mood Indigo' and they named their festival after that song.

WORD BLOCK

Solve the word block puzzle, and find the word hidden in the yellow squares.

1. A college named their festival inspired by his song.

2. Another name for Ganpati.

3. A public ground where people come to honour Dr Ambedkar.

4. They run this for charity.

5. A colour in a rainbow and also the name of a college event

6. Another name for Krishna.

7. The Maharashtrian new year.

8. A street-side festival that means Black Horse.

Write the hidden word here.

GAME TIME

We love quizzes. We're going to see who can get the most points fastest. Come on. You can answer too!

LET'S GET QUIZZICAL

Now that you know all there is to know about Mumbai, can you answer this Mumbai quiz? If you get all of the answers right, then you can be an honorary Mumbaikar. Tick the right answer and see how many you get right.

1. The washerman's steps.
   ◯ Dhobi Ghaat   ◯ Dhobi Jagaha   ◯ Dhobi Salan

2. A market of thieves.
   ◯ Chor Nagari   ◯ Chor Bazaar   ◯ Chor Market

3. The Gateway of India was built to welcome this king.
   ◯ George IV   ◯ George V   ◯ George VI

4. A delicious roll of chapatti stuffed with meat or vegetable curry.
   ◯ Johnny   ◯ Frankie   ◯ Bobby

5. Their cafés are famous in Mumbai.
   ◯ Persian   ◯ Iranian   ◯ Greek

6. These docks are where fish is unloaded.

   ◯ Massoon   ◯ Prasoon   ◯ Sassoon

7. A fountain is named after her.

   ◯ Cora   ◯ Flora   ◯ Dora

8. This slum is one of Asia's largest.

   ◯ Saravi   ◯ Dharavi   ◯ Garavi

9. They came, they saw, they conquered and then gave Mumbai as a wedding gift to their princess.

   ◯ The Spanish   ◯ The British   ◯ The Portuguese

10. This gate lets in trains.

    ◯ Track Gate   ◯ Huffington Gate   ◯ Churchgate

11. This famous writer was born in Mumbai.

    ◯ Lewis Carroll   ◯ Rudyard Kipling   ◯ Enid Blyton

12. This market has just about everything you need.

    ◯ Waterford Market   ◯ Crawford Market   ◯ Stanford Market

DAADU'S DETECTIVE TRAIL

Write the letters here as you find them across the book.

Can you mix up all the letters to form the word?

ANSWERS

page 13 RHYME AWAY

arc, ark, bark, dark, hark, lark, mark, shark, spark, stark

page 15 SHIP SHAPE

page 25 MATCH IT

Sassoon—Docks; Hutatma—Chowk; Church—Gate; Crawford—Market; Flora—Fountain

page 31 HIDDEN WORDS

Here are some of the words that you can form: aim, ham, hat, him, hit, mat, wit, hawk, kiwi, wait, wham, what, whim

page 37 BUS FUSS

A and D are exactly alike.

page 39 WHAT'S ODD?

car, football field, chimney

page 45 JUMBLE TUMBLE

1. cricket   2. chawls   3. Film   4. Dalal

page 47 FOODOKU

page 49 CHAI TIME

page 51 ODD ONE OUT

spinach, cucumber, grocer, cabbage, pea

page 57 TWIN GUDIS

A and D are exactly alike.

page 59 WORD BLOCK

1. Frank Sinatra
2. Ganesha
3. Shivaji Park
4. Marathon
5. Indigo
6. Govinda
7. Gudi Padva
8. Kala Ghoda
Hidden Word: FESTIVAL

page 60 LET'S GET QUIZZICAL

1. Dhobi Ghaat
2. Chor Bazaar
3. George V
4. Frankie
5. Iran
6. Sassoon
7. Flora
8. Dharavi
9. The Portuguese
10. Churchgate
11. Rudyard Kipling
12. Crawford Market

DAADU'S DETECTIVE TRAIL

D A B B A W A L A